Zen Prayers for Repairing Your Life

Also by Tai Sheridan
www.taisheridan.com

Buddha in Blue Jeans Contemplative Series

Buddha in Blue Jeans: An Extremely Short Zen Guide to Being Buddha
Relax...You're Going to Die
Secrets of True Happiness
Zen Prayers for Repairing Your Life

Buddhist Classics in Modern Verse

Celestial Music: Sutras of Emptiness
The Lotus / Diamond / Heart-Wisdom / Loving Kindness Sutras

The Bare Bones Dhammapada: Big Mind Big Love
Buddha's Essential Teachings

The Buddhacarita: A Modern Sequel
The Poetic Saga of Buddha's Life From Birth to Enlightenment

The Zen Wheel of Life Mantra: A Song of Luminous Wisdom and Love
Based on the Bhavacakra - The Wheel of Life Mandala

Zen Classics in Modern Verse

The Light of the Ancient Buddhas: Ballads of Emptiness and Awakening
Based on Keizan's Transmission of the Light

Rice Eyes: Enlightenment in Dogen's Kitchen
A poetic version of Dogen's Tenzo Kyokun on enlightened living and practice

Snow Falling in Moonlight: Odes in Praise of Dogen's Shobogenzo
Twelve Poems based on Dogen's Shobogenzo:The Treasury of the True Dharma Eye

Warm Zen Practice: A Poetic Version of Dogen's Bendowa
Whole Hearted Way

Collections and Other Works

Buddha's Golden Light: Ancient Wisdom in Modern Verse
Patanjali: Yoga Sutras in Lingo: The Liberation of Spirit in Modern Metaphors

Zen Prayers for Repairing Your Life

by Tai Sheridan, Ph.D.

Copyright © 2012 Tai Sheridan

ISBN-13:978-1478235750
ISBN-10:1478235756

Website: www.taisheridan.com
Email: tai@taisheridan.com

Table of Contents

Dedicated to Thomas Merton
and his seeds of contemplation

In the last analysis, the individual person is responsible for living his own life and for "finding himself." If he persists in shifting his responsibility to somebody else, he fails to find out the meaning of his own existence.

- Thomas Merton

Introduction

I offer this book of Zen prayers to help you address what is unsettled within you, to help you cultivate integrity and virtue, and to help you to discover how to bring benefit to life. Prayer can release you from your habitual self-centered tendencies and can open the gates to your miraculous and wondrous existence.

People often associate Zen with difficult meditation practices, arduous training, arcane paradoxes, profound spiritual experiences, and Asian philosophy. In fact, Zen is an experiential return to what is most simple, basic, and universal in your daily life. Regardless of your ethnicity, cultural background, or religious affiliation, these Zen prayers offer an experience of spiritual realization through personal insight and intimacy with life.

All schools and sects of Buddhism include sacred liturgy, invocation, recitation, and prayer as meaningful spiritual practices. Zen prayer is many things, including intimacy with the ground of Being, making yourself whole through honest and humble self-reflection, clarifying your deepest spiritual intentions, cultivating the wish for the welfare of the world, and affirming the essential goodness of people and life.

Prayer invites you to the timeless and infinite border of the material and invisible world, the place where phenomena and emptiness dynamically interact in the dance of existence. Through sound and silence, prayer invokes goodness, healing, mystery, blessings, and can ignite the flame of your heart.

May you dwell in prayer moment after moment.

Tai Sheridan
Kentfield, California
July, 2012

Prayers for Being Buddha

Prayer for Breath

I open myself
to breathing naturally
through the moments
of my life and
with each breath
entering gentle
awareness presence

I am ready
to inhale naturally
and to experience
the depths of
welcoming and
engaging with
all aspects of life

I am ready
to exhale naturally
and to experience
the depths of
letting go and
of allowing life
to flow

I am ready
to discover how
I tighten my body
when I breathe
and resist my
own experience
of present reality

I open myself
to breathing naturally
through the moments
of my life and
with each breath
entering gentle
awareness presence

Prayer for Clarity

I open my mind
to seeing clearly
the essence of things
that matter to me
without being confused
by the muddy waters
of passionate attachment

I am ready
to release myself
from the whirlwinds
of obsession and
mental confusion
which keep me
from seeing clearly

I am ready
to release myself
from mistaking
thinking and analysis
for the deep clarity
of my heart body
and mind

I am ready
to release myself
from fearing
the truth of reality
over the preferences
that shackle and
blind me

I open my mind
to seeing clearly
the essence of things
that matter to me
without being confused
by the muddy waters
of passionate attachment

Prayer for Embodiment

I open myself
to loving my body
as the miracle of
my own life
and as the ground
of my integrity
and spiritual life

I am ready
to delight
in all of my
bodily senses
as a means of
connecting to nature
and humanity

I am ready
to care for
and nourish
my body so
it is vital
and of benefit
to all life

I am ready
to rid myself
of all shame
and guilt that
I have accumulated
about my appearance
and my body

I open myself
to loving my body
as the miracle of
my own life
and as the ground
of my integrity
and spiritual life

Prayer for Loving Kindness

I open my heart
like a lotus blossom
waiting in silence
for boundless love
to fill my pores
and like the sun
warm the world

I am ready to
release myself
from hungering
after people as if
their love will
save me from
my suffering

I am ready to
release myself
from my jealousy
of the love
other's share
and which I miss
during lonely hours

I am ready to
release myself
from thinking that
love can be found
outside of myself
and that my own
heart is empty

I open my heart
like a lotus blossom
waiting in silence
for boundless love
to fill my pores
and like the sun
warm the world

Prayer for Now

I open myself
to being alert
in the present moment
and to being
completely alive
and responsive
to whatever happens

I am ready
to stop avoiding
my experiences
and internal states
of thought emotion
sensation and intuition
as they occur

I am ready
to slow down
so that I can
be centered
within myself
and live close
to the bone

I am ready
to give up
acting as if
past memory
and future wishes
are a satisfying substitute
for right now

I open myself
to being alert
in the present moment
and to being
completely alive
and responsive
to whatever happens

Prayer for Today

I open myself
to today as
the whole
of my life
for it includes
all my experience
my living dying

I am ready
to dive into
today's moments
with vitality clarity
and good will
and to use myself up
without hesitation

I am ready
to stop living
in yesterday
and tomorrow
for it is within
today that the
world blossoms

I am ready
to embrace
everything that
presents itself
for these are
my blessings

I open myself
to today as
the whole
of my life
for it includes
all my experience
my living dying

Prayers for Cultivating Virtue

Prayer for Balance

I open to
being balanced
in my thoughts
emotions speech
and actions so
that harmony
will prevail

I am ready
to catch myself
falling out of
balance by
paying attention
to the experience
of my body

I am ready to
transform the
passions energies
that throw me
and to carefully
observe my reactions
to people events

I am ready to
return to balance
by sensing my
feet on the ground
and by breathing
and centering
in my belly

I open to
being balanced
in my thoughts
emotions speech
and actions so
that harmony
will prevail

Prayer for Contact

I open myself
to genuine contact
with each person
I meet and
to treating them
with utmost respect
and genuine responsiveness

I am ready
to stop protecting
myself from closeness
with other people
by insisting on
my point of view
and by not listening

I am ready
to stop protecting
myself from closeness
with other people
through judgment
discrimination blame
and distancing

I am ready
to stop protecting
myself from closeness
with other people
by withdrawing from them
or by overwhelming them
with my actions

17

I open myself
to genuine contact
with each person
I meet and
to treating them
with utmost respect
and genuine responsiveness

Prayer for Ethics

I open myself
to ethical conduct
based on realizing
that all people
are my own
Buddha body
and true being

I am ready
to speak and act
with high regard
for my own dignity
and to respect myself
when I interact
with the world

I am ready
to speak and act
with clear awareness
and high regard
for the sacred dignity
of all people
and all forms of life

I am ready
to make a
sincere effort
to do no harm
whenever possible
each day in
my brief life

I open myself
to ethical conduct
based on realizing
that all people
are my own
Buddha body
and true being

Prayer for Focus

I open
to focusing my
full attention
on whatever is
before me or
within me and
staying present

I am ready
to use my mind
like a laser to
precisely and
intimately experience
the world of
people and things

I am ready
to use my mind
like the open sky
that in vastness
includes all
aspects of
present reality

I am ready
to use my mind
without trying
to control it
or other people
and to allow it
to function naturally

I open
to focusing my
full attention
on whatever is
before me or
within me and
staying present

Prayer for Forgiveness

I open
to forgiveness
toward myself
and others as
the means of
returning to love
integrity harmony

I am ready
to view harm
as a folly
of being human
and to take a
spacious and wise
view when facing it

I am ready
to recognize
when I have
withdrawn my
kindness because
of the harm
I experience

I am ready
to recognize
when I bear
ill will towards
others because
I feel a sense
of injustice

I open
to forgiveness
toward myself
and others as
the means of
returning to love
integrity harmony

Prayer for Generosity

I open to
generosity as
a way of life
for in giving myself
I will find myself
and will benefit
all life

I am ready
to give myself
to each moment
with the fullness
of my presence
and all of my
inner resources

I am ready
to give myself
to each person
with full attention
and respect
and to understand
them deeply

I am ready
to give myself
to the ebb
and flow of
my life without
reservation or
self protection

I open to
generosity as
a way of life
for in giving myself
I will find myself
and will benefit
all life

Prayer for Honesty

I open
to honesty
as the path
of authenticity
in communicating
with the people
in my life

I am ready
for the courage
to face the
truth and consequences
of my actions
in all spheres
of my life

I am ready
to be honest
with myself
about the benefit
I have brought
to myself others
and the world

I am ready
to be honest
with myself
about the harm
I have brought
to myself others
and the world

I open
to honesty
as the path
of authenticity
in communicating
with the people
in my life

Prayer for Humility

I open to
profound humility
based on my valuable
but small place
in the infinite
and timeless
universe

I am ready
to be vulnerable
based on my mortality
and realize
that the miracle
of my life
is a gift

I am ready
to treasure
each person
and thing as
expressions of
an inexplicable
mystery and miracle

I am ready
to live and
breathe from
sincere humility
as I interact with
people and
all forms of life

I open to
profound humility
based on my valuable
but small place
in the infinite
and timeless
universe

Prayer for Integrity

I open
to integrity
as my core
experience and
intention in
living my life
with others

I am ready
to act from
my core integrity
in all relationships
regardless of the
personal consequences
and outcomes

I am ready
to question myself
deeply before I
react to difficult
circumstances and
experiences that
upset me

I am ready
to develop patience
so that I can
listen to my deeper
meanings and those
of others when
making decisions

I open
to integrity
as my core
experience and
intention in
living my life
with others

Prayer for Intuitive Wisdom

I open myself
to my intuition
and attune
to the harmony
between all things
which is miraculous
and unified

I am ready
to go beyond
my thinking
and feeling
and listen to
my deep inner
knowing of reality

I am ready
to stop judging
and criticizing people
as I open
my reservoirs
of attention clarity
to friends

I am ready
to trust my
spontaneous intuition
and temper it
with wise judgement
when responding
to circumstances

I open myself
to my intuition
and attune
to the harmony
between all things
which is miraculous
and unified

Prayer for Light

I open myself
to the light
that is all being
time and space
and that is the fabric
of all existence
and reality

I am ready
to open myself
to the spacious
and infinite being
that is me
and that is
ever present

I am ready
to walk in humility
and grace as the
responsibility of
somebody who
becomes one
with reality

I am ready
to be completely
human and ordinary
in the light
and to avoid
pride arrogance
and self promotion

I open myself
to the light
that is all being
time and space
and that is the fabric
of all existence
and reality

Prayer for Patience

I open to patience
as the way
of encountering
daily difficulty
and of finding
peace in the
present moment

I am ready
to breathe when
feeling frustrated
or when losing
patience with
challenging people
and circumstances

I am ready
to remember
that my sense of
balance and calm
will help resolve
whatever difficulty
I encounter

I am ready
to remember
that patient
listening and
problem solving
come from harmony
within myself

I open to patience
as the way
of encountering
daily difficulty
and of finding
peace in the
present moment

Prayer for Responsibility

I open myself
to responsibility
for the consequences
of my thoughts
words actions
which have visible
and invisible effects

I am ready
to stop making
excuses within
and with others
for the problems
and difficulties
I cause through
my actions

I am ready
to humbly see
my responsibility
for the goodness
of my actions
and the benefit
they bring others

I am ready
to see that
all life is connected
and that everything
I do ripples the
fabric of humankind
and all life

I open myself
to responsibility
for the consequences
of my thoughts
words actions
which have visible
and invisible effects

Prayer for Self Restraint

I open myself
to self restraint
and the ability
to keep myself
in check so that
I will not live
a reactive life

I am ready
to examine
how I act
impulsively or
compulsively
out of deeply
ingrained habits

I am ready
to act thoughtfully
and to consider
the many options
available to me
before I respond
too quickly

I am ready
to end activities
that keep me
from being
balanced in my
body speech
and mind

I open myself
to self restraint
and the ability
to keep myself
in check so that
I will not live
a reactive life

Prayer for Truth

I open
to truth as
the guiding light
in my life and
as the path
of fundamental
integrity and love

I am ready
to gain compassionate
insight into
the depths of
my thoughts
emotions sensations
and intuition

I am ready
to gain compassionate
insight into
the character
and motivations
of the people
in my life

I am ready
to gain compassionate
insight into
the spiritual basis
of all things
that exists in
the universe

I open
to truth as
the guiding light
in my life and
as the path
of fundamental
integrity and love

Prayer for Vitality

I open
to being vital
in my inward life
and outward expression
and to living
each moment
to its fullest

I am ready
to renew myself
each day through
silence prayer
and touching
the ground of
present being

I am ready
to nourish
my body with
food movement
relaxation and
the awakening of
all of my senses

I am ready
to find balance
between vigorous
activity and rest
so that my vital
energy can flow
harmoniously

I open
to being vital
in my inward life
and outward expression
and to living
each moment
to its fullest

Prayers for Accepting Reality

Prayer for Birth

I open myself
to the birth of
everyone and
everything as
the mystery
of living
and being

I am ready
to live in
daily gratitude
for this precious
human life
that is as rare
as an eclipse

I am ready
to honor the
dignity of all
forms of life
as manifestations
of the miracle
of being

I am ready
to see that
everything is
born fresh
and alive in
each moment of
present awareness

I open myself
to the birth of
everyone and
everything
as the mystery
of living
and being

Prayer for Dying

I open myself
to the dying
of loved ones
friends humanity
and all creatures
for this is the
way of life

I am ready
to accept
my own death
as a natural
and welcomed
thread in the fabric
of the great mystery

I am ready
to release all
of my fears
and resistance
to the end
of my earthly
days and nights

I am ready
to keep the
awareness of death
before me so
that my heart
opens to the
depths of living

I open myself
to the dying
of loved ones
friends humanity
and all creatures
for this is the
way of life

Prayer For Illness

I open myself
to illness as
a natural significant
aspect of life
that I can meet
with responsibility
and grace

I am ready
to offer nourishment
comfort blessings
to myself and others
when illness
of any kind
takes root

I am ready
to maintain
my awareness
of the pain
and discomfort
I experience
without fear

I am ready
to heal myself
from within
and without
and to benefit
gratefully from
others care

I open myself
to illness as
a natural significant
aspect of life
that I can meet
with responsibility
and grace

Prayer for Living

I open myself
to living and dying
as the essence of
my life and am
willing to learn
to be a wise
and kind person

I am ready
to give up
all of my
mental habits
that keep me
from living in
the here and now

I am ready
to give up
all of my
emotional habits
that keep me
from living in
total presence

I am ready
to give up
all of my
bodily habits
that keep me
from living in
peace and harmony

I open myself
to living and dying
as the essence of
my life and am
willing to learn
to be a wise
and kind person

Prayer for Old Age

I open myself
to old age
as a natural
precious dignified
stage of life
for all of
humankind

I am ready
to honor elders
by seeing the
essential goodness
within them
and by accepting
them as they are

I am ready
to accept that
I too will age
and lose the
capacity vigor
and appearance
of my youth

I am ready
to live fully
wherever I
find myself
in life so that
old age becomes
meaningful

I open myself
to old age
as a natural
precious dignified
stage of life
for all of
humankind

Prayer for Sorrow

I open myself
to the sorrow
in my heart
and to the many
losses I have
faced which awaken
my grief

I am ready
to stop protecting
myself from
the painful experience
of loss and sorrow
when it shakes me
to my depths

I am ready
to share my
sorrows with others
for finding
comfort and meaning
in the common ground
of human loss

I am ready
to accept loss
as a difficult
yet natural
part of my life
that will always
be present

I open myself
to the sorrow
in my heart
and to the many
losses I have
faced which awaken
my grief

Prayers for Difficulties

Prayer for Animosity

I open my eyes
to the animosity
I hold on to
towards myself
and others and
am willing
to let it go

I am ready
to see clearly
when I make others
wrong for their
thoughts and deeds
and that this
makes me mean

I am ready
to see clearly
that focusing on
the wrong deeds
of others takes
me outside of
my own skin

I am ready
to see clearly
that I am responsible
and there is nobody
to blame for what
goes on inside of me

I open my eyes
to the animosity
I hold on to
towards myself
and others and
am willing
to let it go

Prayer for Doubt

I open
to seeing
that my doubt
interferes with
having faith
in myself
and my life journey

I am ready
to put my
doubts aside
so that I can
listen to my
intuition and
my true interests

I am ready
to stop listening
to doubts
that interfere
with my spiritual
interests and a life
of loving kindness

I am ready
to creatively doubt
the advice of others
so that I can
consider and explore
the world using
my own wisdom

I open
to seeing
that my doubt
interferes with
having faith
in myself
and my life journey

Prayer for Fear

I open
to acknowledging
my deepest fears
and to transforming
them into courage
for engaging with
life as it arises

I am ready
to accept fear
as a real part
of my life without
judging myself
as deficient or
less than whole

I am ready
to explore the
roots of my fears
so that I can
know myself deeply
and learn about
my vulnerability

I am ready
to stop being
frozen by fear
and to awaken
my breath and
vital energy so
that I live freely

I open
to acknowledging
my deepest fears
and to transforming
them into courage
for engaging with
life as it arises

Prayer for Foolishness

I open
to seeing my
own foolishness
which interferes
with living a
wise kind open
beneficial life

I am ready
to refrain from
actions that interfere
with harmonizing
with the people
and circumstances
I encounter

I am ready
to see how
my self centered
foolishness is
insensitive and
causes harm to
myself and others

I am ready
to transform
my foolishness
into wholesome
thought and action
so that I can live
in unity and harmony

I open
to seeing my
own foolishness
which interferes
with living a
wise kind open
beneficial life

Prayer for Hunger

I open myself
to the hunger
of the world
and to the lack
of true nourishment
that is as palpable
as the air I breathe

I am ready
to acknowledge
my own deep
hungers that
keep me despairing
and are the roots
of many bad habits

I am ready
to bear witness
to the deep
hungers in others
and to be moved
in my heart
toward compassion

I am ready
to feed myself
and the world
with the food
of wisdom love
and beneficial action
to alleviate hunger

I open myself
to the hunger
of the world
and to the lack
of true nourishment
that is as palpable
as the air I breathe

Prayer for Laziness

I open to
the dynamic
energy of my body
and the universe
as I search
for wisdom love
and a spiritual life

I am ready
to catch myself
being lazy and
avoiding the silence
that awakens me
and reveals my
deep inner life

I am ready
to continually learn
about myself
others situations
and viewpoints
in becoming
intimate and kind

I am ready
to renew my
spiritual journey
on a daily basis
so that my life
is a commitment
to truth and being

I open to
the dynamic
energy of my body
and the universe
as I search
for wisdom love
and a spiritual

Prayer for Possessiveness

I open myself
to the ways
I wish to possess
people and things
so that I may feel
secure and safe
in this uncertain world

I am ready
to release myself
from the ways
I try to change
people so that
they will conform
to my needs

I am ready
to release myself
from the ways
I treat people
as objects and
trample their
dignity

I am ready
to release myself
from the habit
of losing myself
to things I want
and giving away
my inner calm

I open myself
to the ways
I wish to possess
people and things
so that I may feel
secure and safe
in this uncertain world

Prayer for Self Centeredness

I open myself
to discovering
my self centered
thoughts and actions
which alienate
me from my
true life

I am ready
to stop acting
as if I am
the center of
the world
and somebody
of great importance

I am ready
to stop believing
that I am better
than anybody else
or that my abilities
give me the right
to judge others

I am ready
to stop being
prideful as
a means of
self protection
and of separating myself
from the common ground

I open myself
to discovering
my self centered
thoughts and actions
which alienate
me from my
true life

Prayer for Withdrawal

I open myself
to acknowledging
I withdraw from
people and events
that bother me
so that I can
feel safe within

I am ready
to release myself
from the habit
of not dealing
with people
and events that
feel uncomfortable

I am ready
to stop turning away
from sensations
and feelings that
are difficult for me
to experience
and understand

I am ready
to quit running
from life's
difficult moments
and hiding
in my cocoon
of self protection

I open myself
to acknowledging
I withdraw from
people and events
that bother me
so that I can
feel safe within

Prayer for Worry

I am open
to letting life
unfold without
worry and agitation
which interfere
with trusting myself
and my life path

I am ready
to catch myself
worrying about things
and to return to
my connection with
the present moment
and real experience

I am ready
to experience worry
as an invitation
to realistic
problem solving
that deals with
my difficulties

I am ready
to transform worry
into true happiness
that accepts the
insecurities and
ambiguities of life
as natural friends

I am open
to letting life
unfold without
worry and agitation
which interfere
with trusting myself
and my life path

Prayers for Bringing Benefit

Prayer for Benefiting Life

I open to
living for the
benefit of all
life and to
working diligently
to bring harmony
to everyone

I am ready
to let go of
my self centered
ways of acting
so that I can
focus on benefiting
all life

I am ready
to keep my needs
simple in order to
bring benefit
to the people
and circumstance
I encounter

I am ready
to take good
care of my life
so that I can
be present and
vital for the
benefit of all

I open to
living for the
benefit of all
life and to
working diligently
to bring harmony
to everyone

Prayer for Community

I open
to community
as the living
body of my life
and as my
true home
and refuge

I am ready
to join in
community activities
as a means of
enjoyment benefit
learning and
enduring intimacy

I am ready
to open to
feedback I
receive from
community friends
as important insight
into myself

I am ready
to be humble
in my dealings
with community
in order to find
my true place
on the wheel of life

I open
to community
as the living
body of my life
and as my
true home
and refuge

Prayer for Forgetting Myself

I open to
forgetting myself
so that all things
become myself
and my true nature
as a cosmic being
comes forward

I am ready to
forget myself
and throw myself
into activity without
self-centered attachments
and the need for
attention or recognition

I am ready to
live in the integrity
of each activity
without attachment
to goals outcomes
personal payoffs
success or failure

I am ready to
live each moment
mindfully with
clear awareness
of things as they are
without projecting
my world view

I open to
forgetting myself
so that all things
become myself
and my true nature
as a cosmic being
comes forward

Prayer for Friendship

I open
to friendship
with myself
and others
as the matrix
of being alive
and spiritual

I am ready
to befriend myself
as the basis
of love insight
contentment knowledge
spirituality and
benefiting life

I am ready
to befriend all
as the basis
of living my
spiritual wisdom
and as the purpose
of being human

I am ready
to vow that
I will not abuse
my power or violate
the integrity of
all human beings
on the earth

I open
to friendship
with myself
and others
as the matrix
of being alive
and spiritual

Prayer for Intertwining

I open myself
to the intertwining
of all people
and all existing things
as the true essence
of my life
and reality

I am ready
to continually cultivate
this awareness of intimacy
and to remember
that I do not exist
as a separate person
or only within myself

I am ready
to continually learn
how to act and speak
in accordance with
my understanding
of everything as
a part of myself

I am ready
to establish a healthy
sense of myself
and my boundaries
so I can be whole
and act skillfully
within the great unity

I open myself
to the intertwining
of all people
and all existing things
as the true essence
of my life
and reality

Prayer for Self Study

I open to
studying myself
by staying alert
to real experience
and by observing
how I move
talk think

I am ready
to live close
to the bone
and to dive
deep within
body emotion
sensation and
my mind

I am ready
to examine
the myriad
personal identifications
I use to substantiate
myself as separate
and apart

I am ready
to observe
how I treat
others and
the world
as if we are
not intertwined

I open to
studying myself
by staying alert
to real experience
and by observing
how I move
talk think

Prayer For Sympathetic Oneness

I open
to walking
in everyone's shoes
and empathizing
with their lives
recognizing them
as my own

I am ready
to witness
the people that
I meet in life
and to listen
to their deepest
views and experiences

I am ready
to have insight
into the multiple
facets of each
person's circumstances
and to respond
with kind empathy

I am ready
to maintain
the integrity of
my own life
and not confuse
another life for mine
as unity manifests

I open
to walking
in everyone's shoes
and empathizing
with their lives
recognizing them
as my own

A Wish for the World

May All Beings Be Happy!

May All Beings Be One!

May All Beings Be Free!

About the Author

Tai Sheridan, Ph.D., is a poet and Zen priest with forty-three years of training in the Shunryu Suzuki lineage. His poetry transforms ancient Buddhist texts into accessible and inspirational verse. The Buddha in Blue Jeans series presents a modern contemplative approach to spiritual awakening. Tai lives in Marin County, California, where he has raised his four children.

Made in the USA
Lexington, KY
19 May 2016